# Dad
# and I

Story and photographs by

Liz Garza-Williams

HAMPTON-BROWN BOOKS
MANY CULTURES, MANY LANGUAGES…MANY POSSIBILITIES!™

Dad puts on his pants.
I put on my pants.

Dad puts on his shirt.
I put on my shirt.

Dad puts on his boots.
I put on my boots.

Dad puts on his jacket.
I put on my jacket.

Dad puts on his hat.
I put on my hat.

Dad puts on a show.
And so do I!